STERLING CHILDREN'S BOOKS
New York

An Imprint of Sterling Publishing Co., Inc.
1166 Avenue of the Americas
New York, NY 10036

ISBN 978-1-4549-2235-3

Distributed in Canada by Sterling Publishing Co., Inc.
c/o Canadian Manda Group, 664 Annette Street
Toronto, Ontario, Canada M6S 2C8
Distributed in the United Kingdom by GMC Distribution Services
Castle Place, 166 High Street, Lewes, East Sussex, England BN7 IXU
Distributed in Australia by NewSouth Books
45 Beach Street, Coogee, NSW 2034, Australia

For information about custom editions, special sales, and premium and corporate purchases,
please contact Sterling Special Sales at 800-805-5489 or specialsales@sterlingpublishing.com.

Illustrations by Elissa Josse and Bethany Robertson
Manufactured in China

Lot #:
2 4 6 8 10 9 7 5 3 1
01/17

www.sterlingpublishing.com

www.curiousjanecamp.com

CURIOUS JANE

science

+

design

+

engineering
for inquisitive girls

STERLING CHILDREN'S BOOKS
New York

We are building a community of confident, inquisitive girls.

Hi! I'm Samantha. I launched Curious Jane eight years ago to give my girls—and *all* girls—a chance to tinker, create, invent, and have fun!

Curious Jane started as a little summer camp in Brooklyn for my daughters and their friends. I drove the camp van, collected lots of fun supplies, and led the projects each day. We made it up as we went along! We had a blast and learned a ton.

Curious Jane has grown a lot since then, and the biggest thing I gained from that first summer is that the best way to create something, to build something, to try something . . . is to just jump in and ***make*** it. Give it a go, and see what happens!

Making things with my hands is my favorite thing to do—I like to make objects that move, projects that look beautiful, things that are colorful, clever, smart, and funny. No matter what we are working on at Curious Jane, the team often hears me say "Get out of your head and let your hands do the thinking!"

This is our first book, and we are SUPER excited to share some of our favorite projects with you. These pages are packed with activities on science + design + engineering for cool, creative girls like you!

Our projects are all about using what you have at hand. You don't need fancy materials, special tools, or sophisticated techniques. You can do a lot with the everyday objects around you, and we hope this book will inspire you to see common objects in new ways. I want you to open your kitchen drawer and see aluminum foil as a conductive element (electric quiz board, anyone?), to see an embroidery hoop as your own screen-printing frame, and to build an impressive weight-bearing bridge out of cord and cardboard. It's fun to use all of your imagination!

Happy Making!

Samantha

Contents

stay curious

hooray!

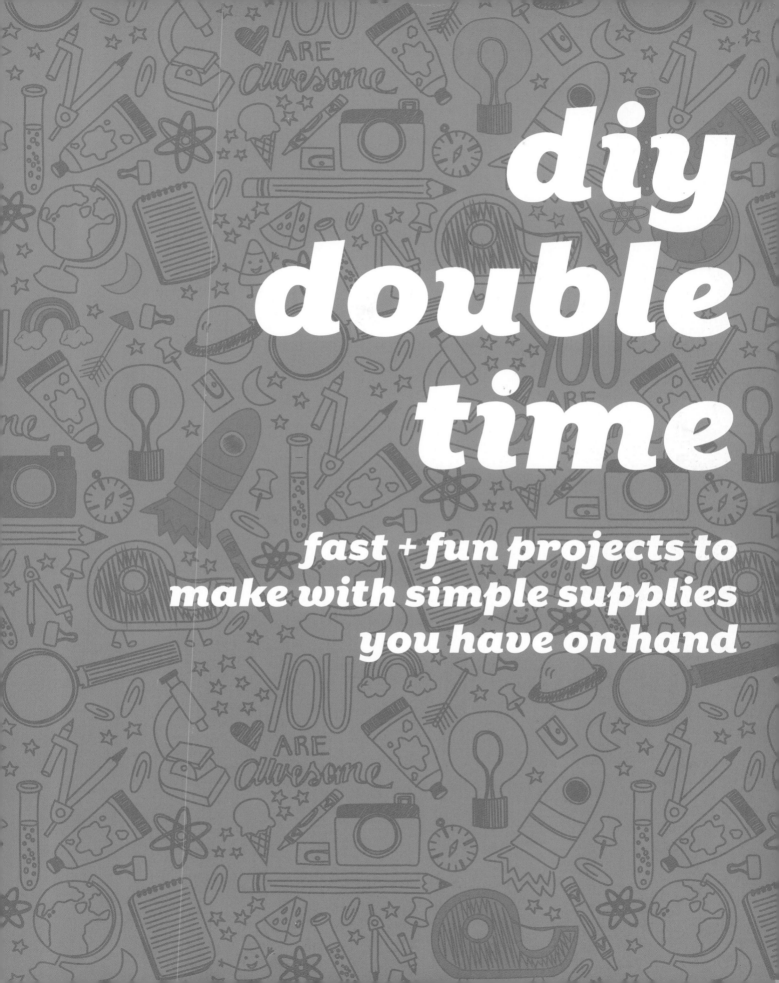

diy double time

fast + fun projects to make with simple supplies you have on hand

cloud in a jar

make a cloud in a jar? sure!

Via Steve Spangler, a science guy we like, we found a couple of projects to help you do just that. (See more of his fun projects here: www.SteveSpanglerScience.com.)

two ways to make your own clouds
try this one on your own

maker checklist

a large glass jar + a small glass of water

foam shaving cream, any brand

a pipette or medicine dropper

blue food coloring

BLUE
Liquid Food Coloring

Professional Quality for the Home Kitchen

Fl. Oz. (29.5 ml)

1 Fill your jar a little more than halfway full with water, then squirt the foam shaving cream all over the top so it completely covers the surface of the water.

2 Using your pipette or dropper, dribble small streams of water on top of your shaving cream cloud. When the dribbled water starts making small streams through your cloud, switch to food coloring; drip it on top, and watch your rainstorm form.

maker checklist

a large glass jar

a saucer that fits on top

hot water

a scoop of ice

food coloring (optional)

a match (with an adult)

1 Start with a large glass jar with a saucer that fits on top like a lid. Put a scoop of ice into the saucer, and, with help, fill your jar halfway with very hot water. Place the saucer and ice on top of the jar, and watch closely as a small cloud forms above the water. You will see it condense and trickle down the inside of the jar like rain.

A·maz·ing

2 Prepare your experiment again. Fill your jar halfway full with hot water, and place a saucer of ice on top. Now have a grown-up helper light the match. Quickly place the tip of the match in between the saucer and the rim of the jar. (The match should be sandwiched between the jar and saucer; do not drop it into the water.) The flame will go out, but the heat from the match will draw a larger cloud up off the water.

3 Once a small cloud has accumulated, take the saucer off of the jar. Watch carefully as the cloud rises up and out. It will look like a miniature patch of fog escaping from your jar.

about clouds...
did you know?

- A cloud is a large group of tiny water droplets that we can see in the air.
- Rain, sleet, snow, and hail falling from clouds is called *precipitation*.
- There are lots of different types of clouds, but the main ones are: *cumulus*, *stratus*, and *cirrus*.
- Fog is actually a cloud that hovers close to the ground!

nature walk bracelet

our new favorite project!

maker checklist

duct tape + scissors

a park, yard, or beach

possibly a friend

your WRIST!

make your own

Just wrap a piece of duct tape around your wrist—sticky-side up!—and go for a walk.

fun!

wishes +
dreams jar

maker checklist

- colorful paper
- pens + pencils
- wishes + dreams
- washi tape
- glass jar
- letter beads + thin cord or string (optional!)

Wishing for something TRULY magical to happen!

xxxxxxxxxxxxxxxxx

 Cut squares of colorful paper and write your favorite big, small, funny, hopeful (you get the picture!) wishes and dreams on them—try fancy lettering and little doodles, too.

2 Roll your papers into tiny scrolls and tape them around the middle with a band of washi tape. Make a nice mix of colors.

tip: Wrap the paper around a pencil, tape it, and then slide it off the pencil.

3 Fill your jar with wishes and dreams! You can save them for years (forever, really!). Read them or share them at any time.

Try it!

We wrapped washi tape around the top of the jar and strung letter beads on thin cord to add color and individuality.

toss-and-talk ball

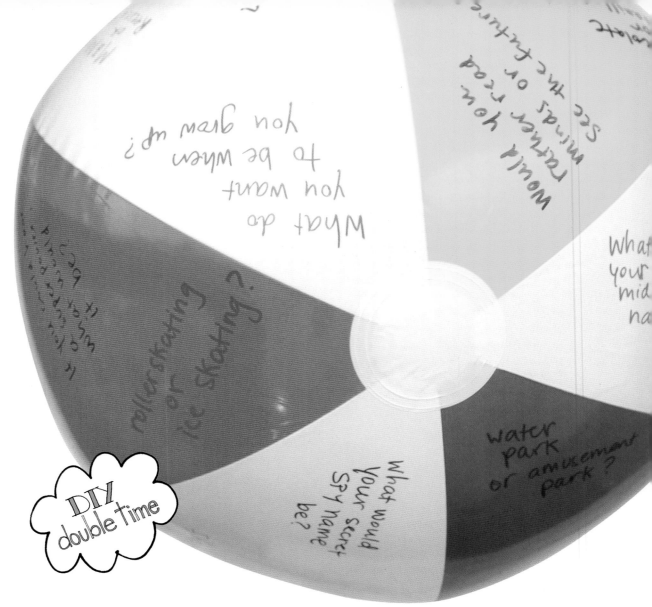

Questions on the ball:
- What do you want to be when you grew up?
- Would you rather read minds or see the future?
- rollerskating or ice skating?
- What would your secret spy name be?
- water park or amusement park?
- What's your middle name?

DIY double time

maker checklist

permanent marker

beach ball

some friends

1 Use a permanent marker to write fun, silly, and thought-provoking questions onto a beach ball.

2 Toss it with friends. When you catch it, read the question that is closest to your right thumb. What's your answer?

here are some questions to get you started!

You're in the circus! Are you a *lion tamer* or a *sword swallower*?

You're going on *vacation*! Where will you go?

Would you rather be able to **fly** or be **invisible**?

If you could only eat **one food** for two weeks, what would it be?

Would you rather have a *pet unicorn* or a *pet dragon*?

If you could have **one wish** granted right now, what would it be?

Cookie or *cupcake*?

What's the *silliest face* you can make?

Water slide or *roller coaster*?

Mountain or **beach**?

What **three words** describe you?

Who do you *admire*?

diy glitter tattoos

i like it

FUN!

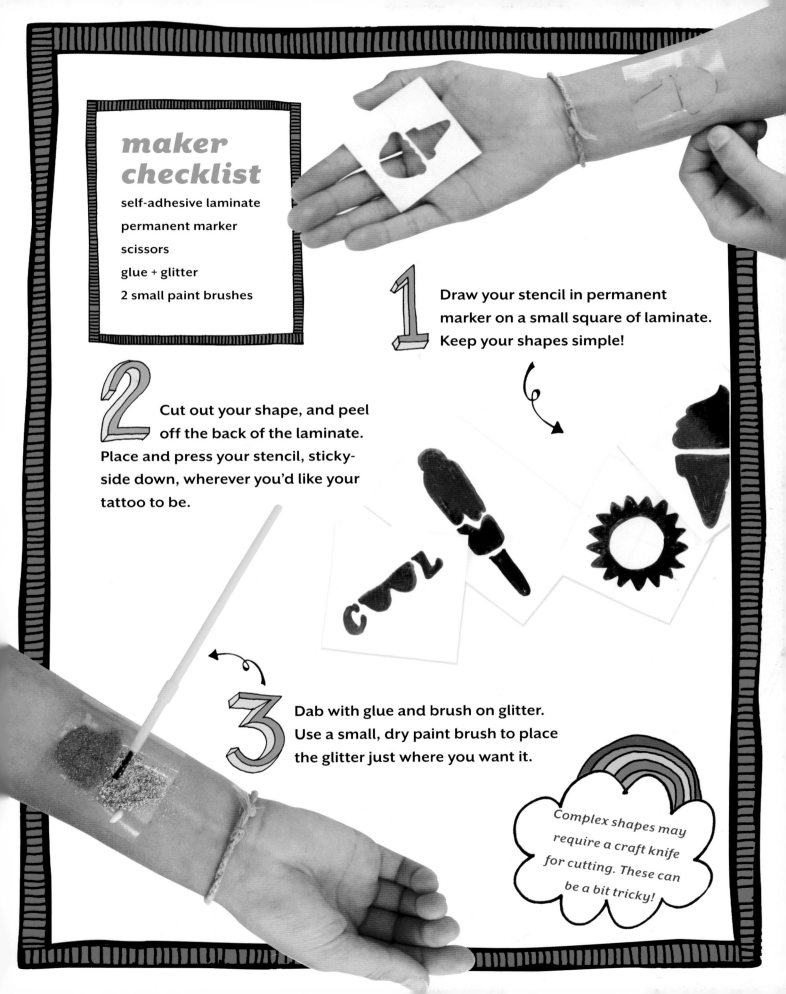

maker checklist

self-adhesive laminate
permanent marker
scissors
glue + glitter
2 small paint brushes

1 Draw your stencil in permanent marker on a small square of laminate. Keep your shapes simple!

2 Cut out your shape, and peel off the back of the laminate. Place and press your stencil, sticky-side down, wherever you'd like your tattoo to be.

3 Dab with glue and brush on glitter. Use a small, dry paint brush to place the glitter just where you want it.

Complex shapes may require a craft knife for cutting. These can be a bit tricky!

washi tape frames

Don't fret! Washi tape is easy to remove and won't leave marks on your walls.

maker checklist

washi tape

artwork you love

First, place your artwork on the wall.
Then tape the frames around it.

Frame your favorite art and photos to make a bold statement.

spa science

mix and fizz your way to these luxe, sweet-smelling, at-home treatments

mix-and-match face scrubs

Choose one option from each group—scrub, soothe, scent, and surprise—and mix your way to a simple face mask!

scrub!

Shed your dry skin by gently buffing your bod with one of these natural exfoliants.

brown sugar

sea salt

coffee

oats

soothe!

Ahhhh . . . Rehydrate your skin with a natural, not-too-heavy moisturizing oil.

ALMOND OIL

OLIVE OIL

coconut oil

Shea butter

yogurt

cocoa butter

scent!

Use a subtle fragrance to add a relaxing element to your spa creation.

cinnamon

rose

chamomile

lavender

cool

PLAY

avocado

vanilla

banana

surprise!

These kitchen staples can add a
fun twist—and a flavor, scent, or key
ingredient—to your spa concoction.

cocoa

honey

Just find your favorite yummy, good-smelling ingredients—things you have on hand in your kitchen pantry—like . . .

oats + brown sugar + honey + banana

blueberries + olive oil + yogurt + oats + sugar

yogurt + avocado + sea salt + dill

. . .and mix them up!

Apply, let the mask sit for a few minutes, and then wash off thoroughly.

peppermint foot scrub

maker checklist

- sugar
- coconut oil
- peppermint essential oil
- vitamin E oil
- food coloring

1 Combine 2 cups sugar with 1 cup coconut oil and mix well.

2 Add 4 to 6 drops of peppermint essential oil and 1 teaspoon vitamin E oil. Stir until combined.

CJ FAVE

SUPERFUN

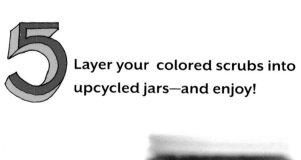

3 Separate mixture into as many bowls as you'd like—next you'll add color.

4 Add food coloring one tiny drop at a time until you get the color you want.
tip: A little goes a long way!

5 Layer your colored scrubs into upcycled jars—and enjoy!

It's fresh and tingly and will make your tired tootsies smell terrific!

shower jellies

maker checklist

1 cup water

large mixing bowl

2 packs unflavored gelatin

½ cup uncolored shower gel

1–2 drops food coloring

3 smaller mixing bowls

stir sticks

silicone cupcake molds

optional but fun:

3–4 drops essential oil

edible glitter

tiny toy to tuck inside

 Boil the water (with grown-up help), and pour into a large mixing bowl.

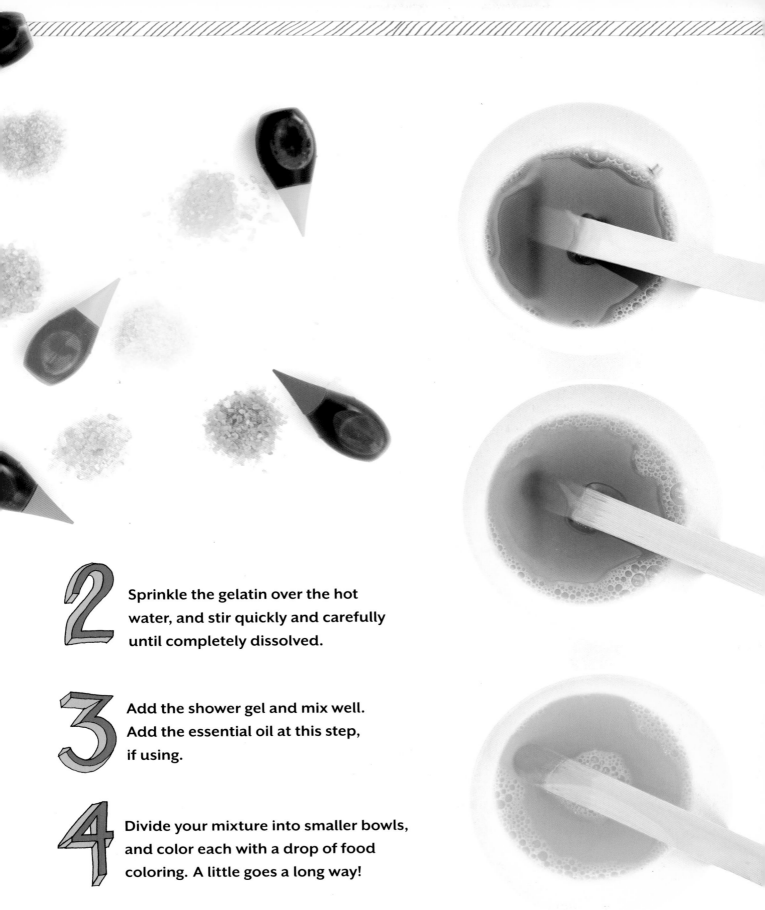

2 Sprinkle the gelatin over the hot water, and stir quickly and carefully until completely dissolved.

3 Add the shower gel and mix well. Add the essential oil at this step, if using.

4 Divide your mixture into smaller bowls, and color each with a drop of food coloring. A little goes a long way!

5 Pour into molds and let set! If you have edible glitter or a tiny toy, you can add it at this step. Then refrigerate to keep cool.

Dust some glitter into your mold or drop in a tiny toy, then fill with your shower jelly mixture.

cool

Edible glitter is smaller and finer than craft glitter, and it's perfectly safe to use on your skin! It's also called disco dust—fun!

AWESOME

Keep your jellies in the fridge so they'll hold their shape until you are ready to use them.

YAY!

cool in the shower
on a hot day!

gem soaps

maker checklist

2–3 bars of solid glycerin

saucepan

food coloring in many colors

paper cups or containers

optional:

essential oils

38

1 Over low heat in a saucepan, slowly melt the bars of glycerin. Make sure to do this with adult help!

attention:
Melt slowly and evenly!

2 Cut down your containers or paper cups so that they are about 2–3 inches tall. The more you have, the more colors you will be able to make!

cool

Make sure the containers can hold hot liquids without leaking!

 Pour the melted glycerin—carefully!—into your containers about 1½ inches in depth. Add food coloring and stir slowly to combine. Let cool completely (about 1 to 2 hours, depending on thickness).

4 Tear the containers away from the hardened soap.

5 Cut the colorful blocks into smaller cubes using a butter knife. Continue to cut the edges at various angles to create light-catching gems!

Geometry is the branch of math that studies points, lines, planes, surfaces, and solids, and the relations between them. As you cut your gem soaps, think about all the shapes you can create.

The intersections of the planes create interesting angles, reflecting light in beautiful ways.

diy flip-flops

maker checklist

- cardstock
- scissors + marker
- colorful craft foam
- rubber cement
- brass brad

1 Create your flip-flop template on a piece of cardstock, like the one we used here.

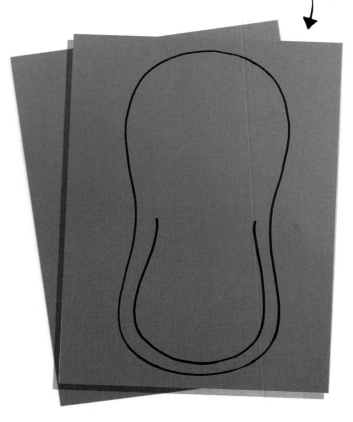

2 Trace your shape onto sheets of craft foam (as many as you like!) and cut them out.

tack down

flip up

cut here

3 For the top layer, cut along this line, fold up, and secure in place with a brad. Just stack, glue, and repeat!

Try it!

favorite colorful fix
Tie water balloons onto your DIY flip-flops or a pair you already have!

bath salts

Make and shake!

1 Measure any mixture of salts into a small container. Add food coloring, dried herbs, and a small drop of essential oil as desired.

2 Seal and shake! Shaking the salt with a drop of food coloring gives the most even coverage.

3 Layer your colored salts in a pretty jar or container. Keep by the bath or give as a gift!

HOW-TO

for colorful layers

Divide your salt mixture into multiple small containers. Add a drop of food coloring to each, and shake to coat. Use a funnel to layer them into a bottle or jar. We used a vinaigrette bottle for our rainbow layers and test tubes for our herbed bath salts.

lavender **chamomile** **rose**

45

fizzy bath bombs

Mix your ingredients and get a chemical reaction!

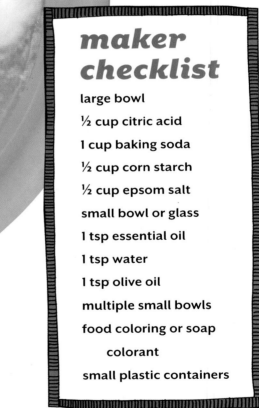

maker checklist

large bowl

½ cup citric acid

1 cup baking soda

½ cup corn starch

½ cup epsom salt

small bowl or glass

1 tsp essential oil

1 tsp water

1 tsp olive oil

multiple small bowls

food coloring or soap
   colorant

small plastic containers

EPSOM SALT

CORN STARCH

BAKING SODA

CITRIC ACID

1 Combine dry ingredients in a large bowl and mix well.

Try it!

SUPERFUN

2

Stir wet ingredients together in a small bowl or glass.

3

Very slowly add the wet mixture to the dry mixture and keep mixing! Mix, mix, mix, so it doesn't fizz and bubble up! After it's all combined, let your mixture sit for a few minutes. It should feel like wet sand and stay together when you squeeze it in your hand. If it's still too dry or crumbly, add a drop of water or olive oil—but be careful not to let it get too wet!

WATER

OLIVE OIL

4 Separate the mixture into smaller bowls and add a drop of food coloring or soap colorant. Mix well! We found mixing by hand was the most effective way to get an even color. It's also nice to leave one bowl white for layering!

Have fun! Experiment with adding a touch of glitter, colored sea salt, tea leaves, or flower petals!

5 Layer your mixture into molds. We used plastic ornaments split in half and experimented with small plastic containers and other recyclables, like yogurt cups.

6 Pack the layers down tightly into the mold by pressing with your fingers.

7 Let dry for a few minutes before *carefully* removing the bath bomb from the mold. Don't try to handle the bath bomb yet! Turn it out from its mold directly onto a surface to dry, and let dry a few hours or overnight.

YAY!

drop in a warm bath and enjoy!

the science behind the fizz!

The main ingredient in bath bombs is the chemical sodium bicarbonate, a.k.a. baking soda. The other key ingredient is citric acid. These chemicals don't do much as dry powders, but in water they react and dissolve to produce tiny bubbles of carbon dioxide gas, which is what causes the fizzzzzzzing! (A similar reaction is commonly used in volcano science projects to create foaming "lava.") The fizzing helps the bath bombs dispense faster and, combined with the hot water, spreads whatever yummy scent you have chosen.

Hide a fun surprise inside your bath bomb, like a mini plastic fish or dinosaur!

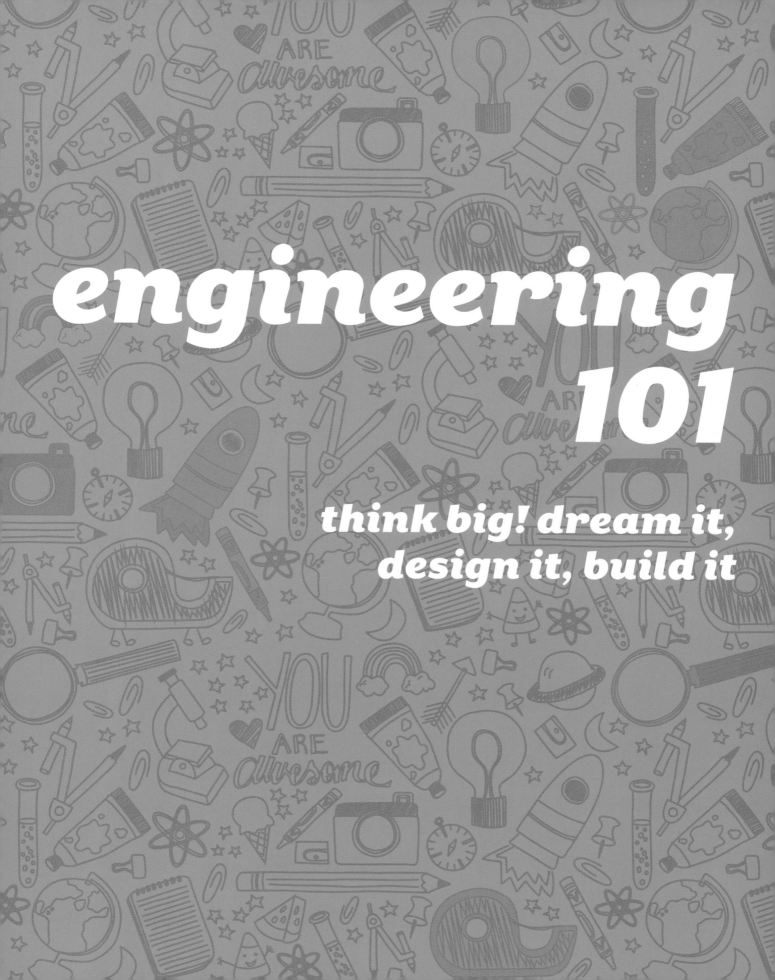

engineering
101

think big! dream it, design it, build it

twinkly fox ears

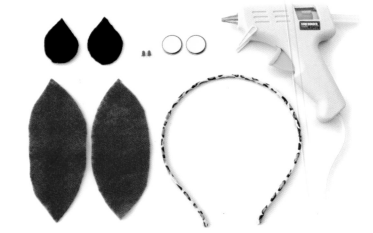

1 Make your ears . . .

Fold a piece of felt in half. Using the fold as the bottom line, cut out two same-size ear shapes. When you unfold the felt, you'll have two pieces that look like the bright-purple felt in our example. Next cut two smaller ear shapes from a single (unfolded) piece of felt. These will be the insides of your ears, like the black felt in our example.

2 Attach to your headband . . .

Fold the large ear shapes back together around your headband and glue them into place. Then glue the small pieces to the front of each ear, in the middle. Make sure not to use too much glue—it will make it hard to push the LEDs through the felt.

3 Add your lights . . . this is a big step . . .

Carefully push the LED legs through the center of each ear. You may need to wiggle the wire legs back and forth a little to get them through. Eventually they will poke through the felt and out the back; this is where you want them.

Position your coin battery between the LED legs so that the bulb lights up. Sandwich the bottom leg between the felt and the battery, and use tape or hot glue to secure it into place. Add a bit of tape to the leg that is sticking up, and voila! When you tape the wire in place, your ear lights up! Repeat with the other ear, and . . .

wear with
joy!

tinker more

draw bot
a scribbling machine

maker checklist

sturdy paper cup

3 skinny markers

masking tape + duct tape

adhesive (sticky dots)

craft decorations

two AAA (1.5 volt) batteries

AAA battery housing with switch

small weight (or magnet)

motor with rotating rod

Mabuchi FA-130 Motor

AWESOME

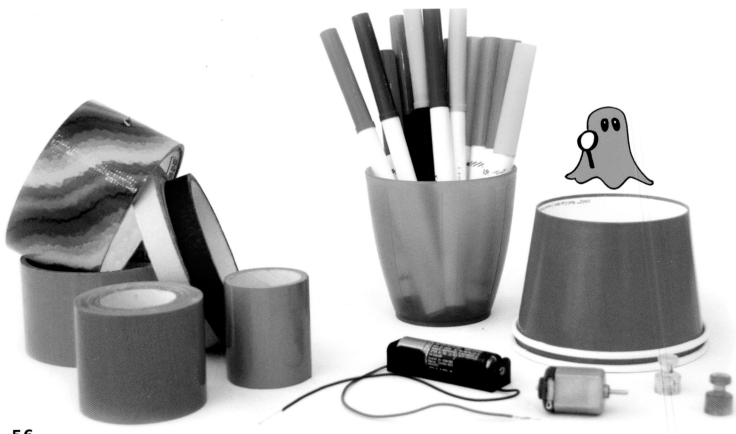

Before you start . . .

Test your components. Place your batteries in the holder (make sure they are in correctly!) and touch the wires to the tiny metal wings on the motor. If the rod doesn't spin, troubleshoot to see if the batteries, holder, or motor need to be replaced.

Don't get shocked!

The red-and-black coating is called *insulation*. The wire is inside. Handle the wires by the insulation whenever the battery is connected.

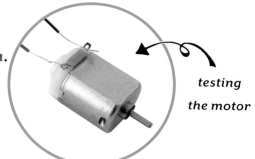

testing the motor

1 Make your tripod! Position the three markers so that they are evenly spaced around the cup and the cup is level. Use small pieces of masking tape to tack the marker legs in place (make sure the caps are pointing down), then secure it, round and round, with duct tape.

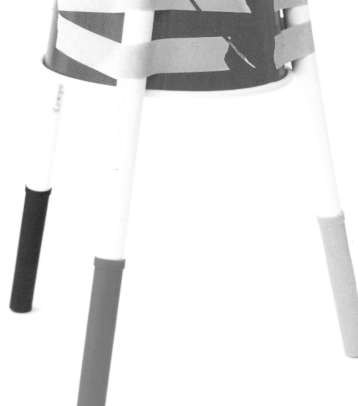

First, tack each marker in place with masking tape, and make sure your bot is even. Then secure the legs with duct tape.

The Eccentric Weight

The key to the drawbot's motion is the eccentric weight that you add to the motor. We used a small magnet, but you can use any small object (like a hex nut) with a little weight. The magnet stays on by itself, but you will need to tape or hot-glue the weight to the rod.

In technical terms, "eccentric" means not placed centrally or off-axis.

the key to how the drawbot works

Without the weight, the motor just spins without causing any disruption. With the weight, the motor spins in an off-balance way, causing the drawbot to wiggle and scribble about. Different size weights produce different patterns.

2 Engineer your circuit. Make sure the battery is off! Your cup should be upside down with the motor and battery on top. Make sure the motor rod fully extends off the edge of the cup and is free to spin without hitting the lip of the cup.

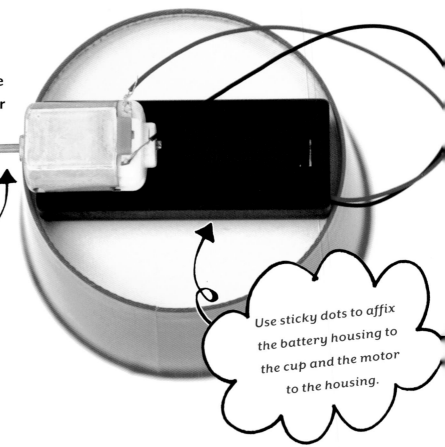

Use sticky dots to affix the battery housing to the cup and the motor to the housing.

You made it to the **FUN** *final step!*

3 Affix the weight, remove the marker caps, and let 'er loose!

YAY!

suspension bridge

maker checklist

cardboard or foam core

two chairs with a space above the seat (folding chairs work great!)

a pile of heavy books

thick + thin cord (or yarn)

scissors + hole punch

masking tape + duct tape

1 Tape your cardboard or foam core together into a long strip (8–10 inches wide by 50–60 inches long).

2 Place the chairs facing away from each other. Span your cardboard or foam core from one seat to the other. Set heavy books on each end to weight them to the seat.

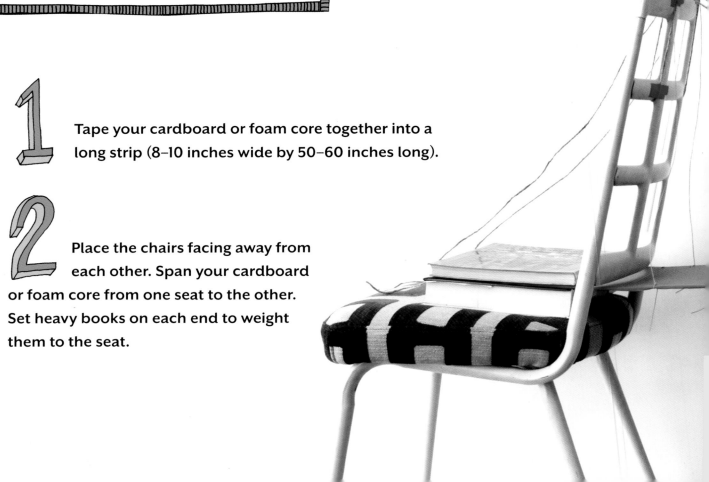

3 Cut two lengths of heavier cord, about 6 feet long. These are your suspension cables. With help, use a hole punch or craft knife to make two holes in each of the far corners of the ends of the cardboard or foam core. Thread the suspension cables through the holes, loop around, and tie securely.

4 Hang your suspension cables by bringing the cord up to the top of the tower, (taping in place on the back of the chair here), drooping it a bit between the towers, taping the cord again where it meets the second tower, and securing it tightly through the opposite end of the deck.

5 Hang your vertical cables by cutting a single piece of cord for your center vertical cable. Tie it to the mid-point of one suspension cable. Loop it under the deck and up the other side. Tie this to the midpoint of the other suspension cable so that the deck is supported.

cool

6 Now cut two pieces of cord, equal in length and a bit longer than your center cable. Follow the same process as before, securing these on either side of the center cable. Keep placing vertical cables in this way until your deck is fully supported. You may need to tweak and adjust as you go. That's ok!

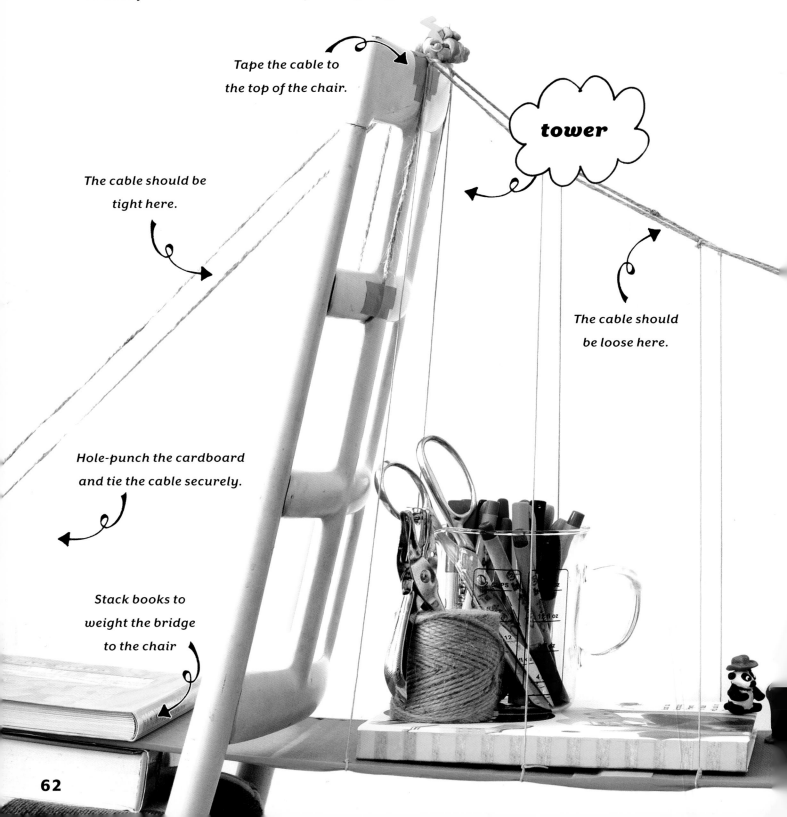

Tape the cable to the top of the chair.

tower

The cable should be tight here.

The cable should be loose here.

Hole-punch the cardboard and tie the cable securely.

Stack books to weight the bridge to the chair

How it works

A suspension bridge is a kind of bridge where the deck (usually a road; ours is cardboard) is hung below suspension cables (your cord or yarn). These long suspension cables are anchored by towers (here, the chairs!) on either end of the bridge. Smaller vertical cables are hung from the long cables, and these hold the deck up.

This type of bridge can support a lot of weight!

suspension cables

vertical cables

deck

inertia zoom ball

Do this with
a friend!

did you know?

The first law of movement is *inertia*—that means an object at rest (not moving) will remain at rest unless something moves it, and an object in motion will remain in motion unless something stops it.

maker checklist

2 large soda bottles

good scissors (or a craft knife)

duct tape or masking tape

2 lengths of cord, each about 12 feet

1 Carefully cut the soda bottles in half.

2 Connect the two top halves with plenty of tape. Decorate!

3 Thread both lengths of cord through the bottle. You have a zoom ball!

A·maz·ing

how to use it

Stand apart from a friend, holding the cord firmly. If the zoom ball is closest to you, pull your cords apart quickly. This will send the zoom ball to your friend. Then bring your hands back together so your friend can send the ball zooming back to you. Get a good rhythm going.

Open • close • open • close!

When you use your arms to transfer energy to the cord, your zoom ball pops into motion, racing from one end of the cord to the other.

a tip we learned:

If the zoom ball gets going really fast, it can hit your knuckles hard. Wear gloves or socks on your hands to protect them and have more fun!

mini catapults

A quick and easy project using a few simple things you have lying around at home.

maker checklist

8 craft sticks

thin masking tape

a few rubber bands

a plastic spoon

plus...

fun little items to launch
from your catapult!

PLAY

1 Stack 6 craft sticks together and tape securely at each end. (You can also use rubber bands instead of tape to secure them.)

Have fun with it!

2 Place another craft stick on top of the stack (positioning it like you see in the picture). Wrap another rubber band around them both—creating a figure X—so that it is nice and tight.

3 Tape your plastic spoon along one more craft stick and lay it across the other side of the stack. Use a rubber band (and a bit of help!) to hold the ends of the two single craft sticks together with the stack in the middle. Now you're ready to launch!

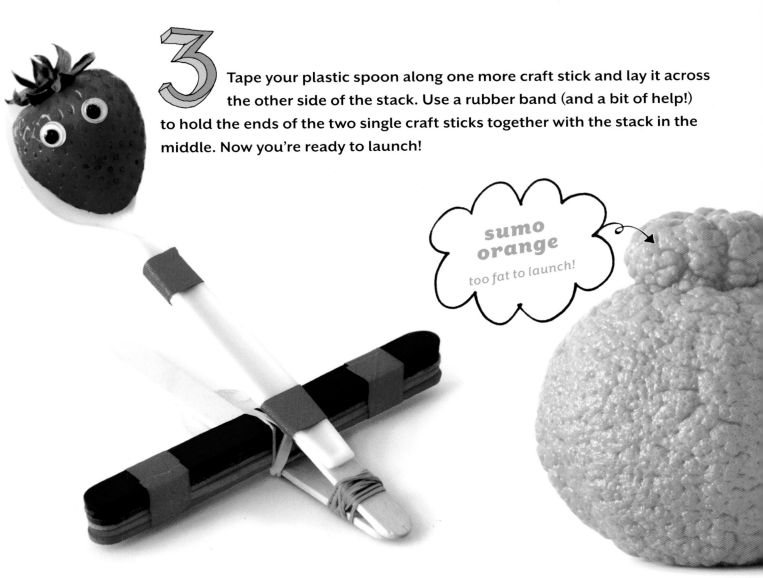

sumo orange

too fat to launch!

wind-up rubber band cars

tinker more

Try this engineering project... and take it outside!

HOW TO

make the body of your car . . .

1 Cut a piece of corrugated cardboard (the kind with the ridges in the middle) into a square, about 5 x 5 inches. Cut a smaller rectangle, about 2 x 1 inches tall, out of one side.

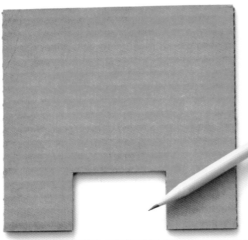

Make sure the ridges are parallel to the edge that you cut! This is the key to the next step.

2 Carefully slide your skewer or thin dowel through one side of the cardboard and out the other, like you see in this picture to the right. The skewer must slide through a space between the ridges so that it will spin freely.

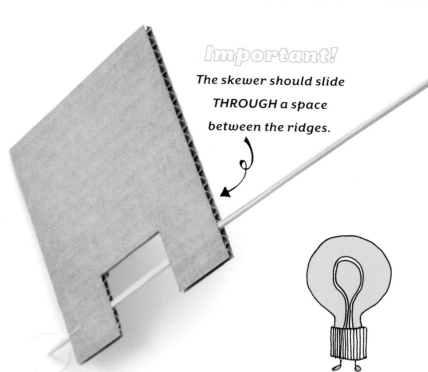

Important!

The skewer should slide THROUGH a space between the ridges.

3 Secure a small rubber band to the top of the cardboard near the edge that is opposite the side with the skewer. We used a few pieces of tape to make sure it stays in place! Wind a piece of tape around the middle of the skewer, leaving a small tab sticking out.

Just tape ONE side of the rubber band. You will need to stretch the other end to meet the skewer.

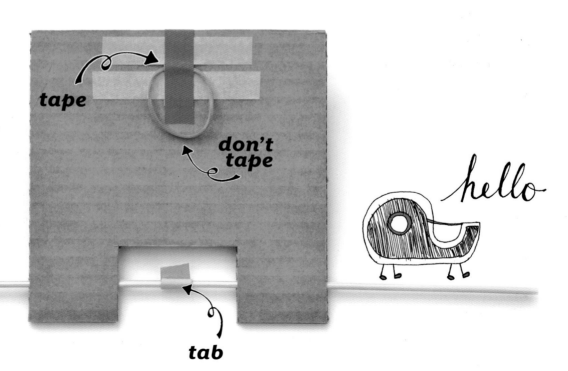

tape

don't tape

hello

tab

HOW TO

make the wheels . . .

super glue

4 First, cut two small squares of cardboard from any scraps you have left over. The squares should be about 1 x 1 inches, or large enough to cover the hole in the CD. Now lay your CDs on a flat surface. Make sure you have a large piece of scrap paper underneath. Use a bit of super glue to glue each square to the center of two of the discs. Let it dry, then glue the other discs on top, lining them up evenly. They should look like sandwiches, with discs on each side and cardboard in the middle.

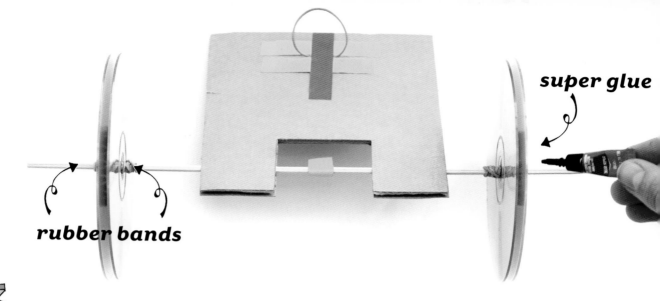

super glue

rubber bands

5 Wind a small rubber band around each end of the skewer, about 1 inch from the cardboard. This will help keep your wheels in place. Now, with help from a grown-up, punch each end of the skewer through the hole (and cardboard) in each CD wheel. Add another rubber band on either side of each wheel to make it more secure. For extra strength, put a bit of super glue where the cardboard in the wheel touches the skewer.

6 Carefully stretch the rubber band forward and around the tape tab. Hold it loosely in place while you turn the dowel. The rubber band will wind around the dowel as you spin it. Set the car on a smooth, flat surface, and let it go!

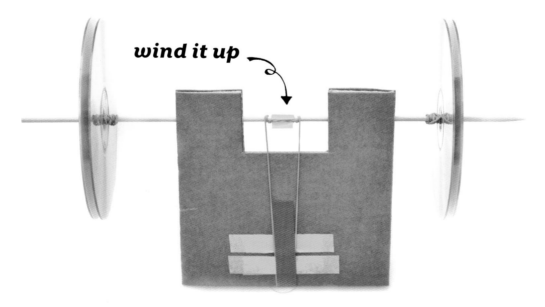

wind it up

wind it up and let it go!

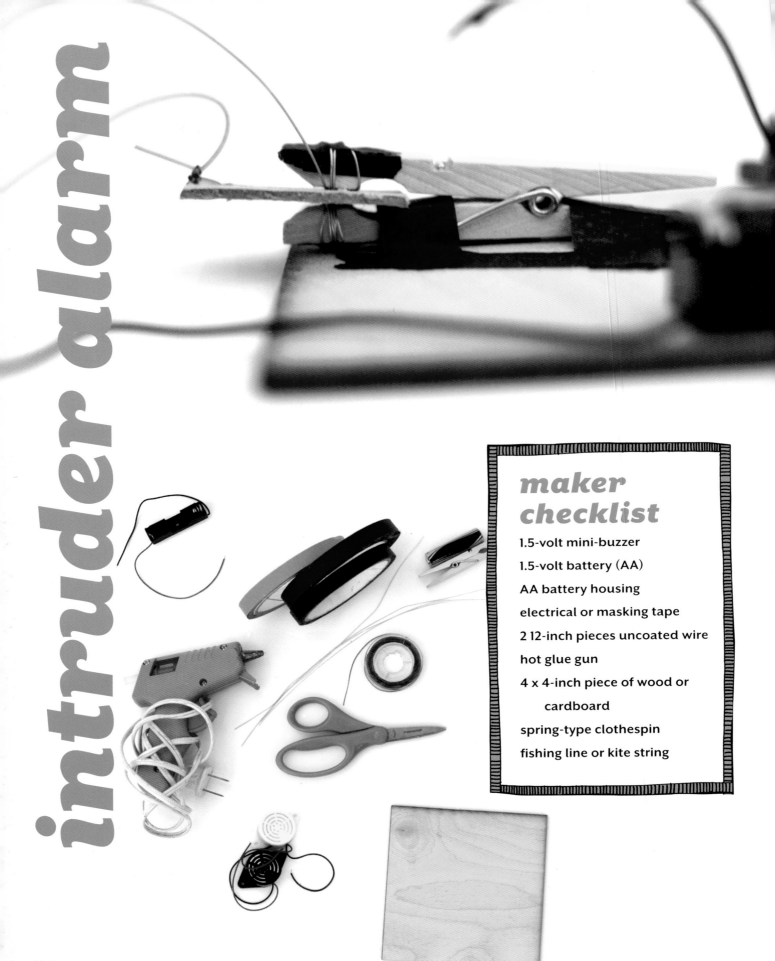

intruder alarm

maker checklist

1.5-volt mini-buzzer

1.5-volt battery (AA)

AA battery housing

electrical or masking tape

2 12-inch pieces uncoated wire

hot glue gun

4 x 4-inch piece of wood or
    cardboard

spring-type clothespin

fishing line or kite string

Before you get started,

test your buzzer by connecting it to the battery, as shown. It should make a sound! No sound? Make sure you've connected the correct ends. If that doesn't work, try a new battery. Still no sound? You may need a new buzzer.

Don't get shocked!

The red and black coating is called insulation. The wire is inside. Handle the wires by the insulation whenever the battery is connected!

Connect the red wire to the positive (+) end and the black wire to the negative (–) end.

1 First, set up your buzzer and battery housing on a scrap of wood or stiff cardboard, as shown. Use hot glue to fix them in place.

twist here

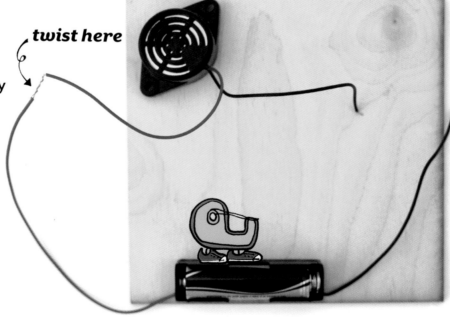

2 Connect the buzzer's red wire to the red wire of the battery housing by twisting the ends together. Make sure the black wires are *not* touching.

Test your components. Holding the two black wires by the insulated portion, touch the metal tips together. This completes the circuit, and the alarm should buzz.

3 Now, take one of your 12-inch pieces of bare wire. Tape one end to the top end of the clothespin and wrap it around 6 to 8 times. Add another bit of tape to the top to secure it, but make sure to leave 2–3 inches of wire sticking out. Do the same to the bottom part of the clothespin. When the clothespin is closed, the wire wrapped around each side should touch.

4 Use masking tape or hot glue to secure the clothespin to the board, like in the picture on the opposite page.

5 *Important:* Remove the battery first! Now connect one wire from the clothespin to the black wire of the alarm. Connect the wire from the other end of the clothespin to the black wire of the battery housing.

Use a bit of tape on the top to secure the wire.
But don't put any tape here.

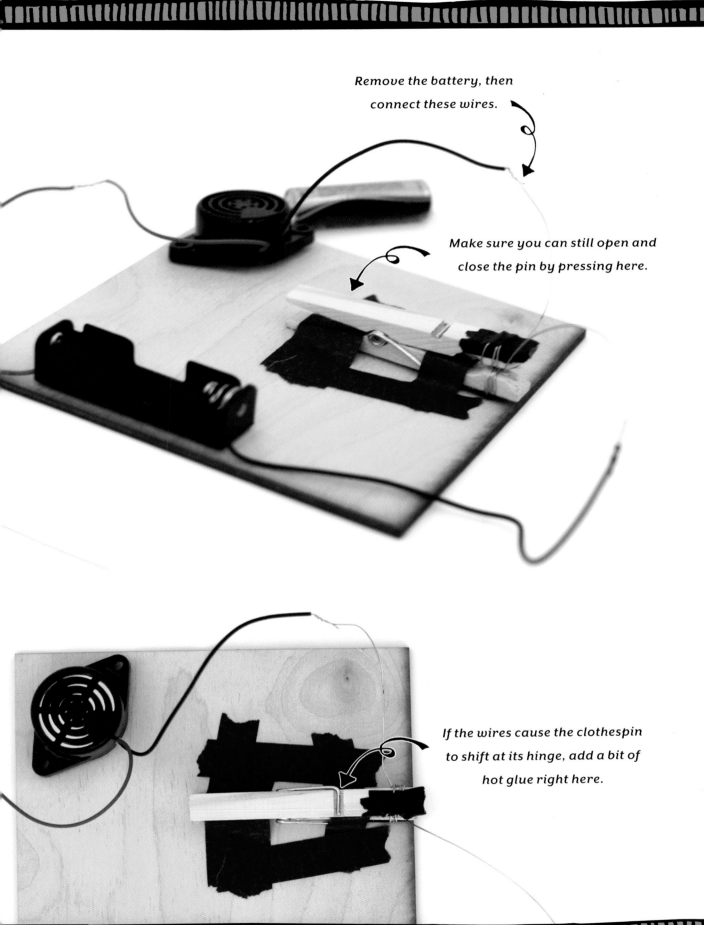

Remove the battery, then connect these wires.

Make sure you can still open and close the pin by pressing here.

If the wires cause the clothespin to shift at its hinge, add a bit of hot glue right here.

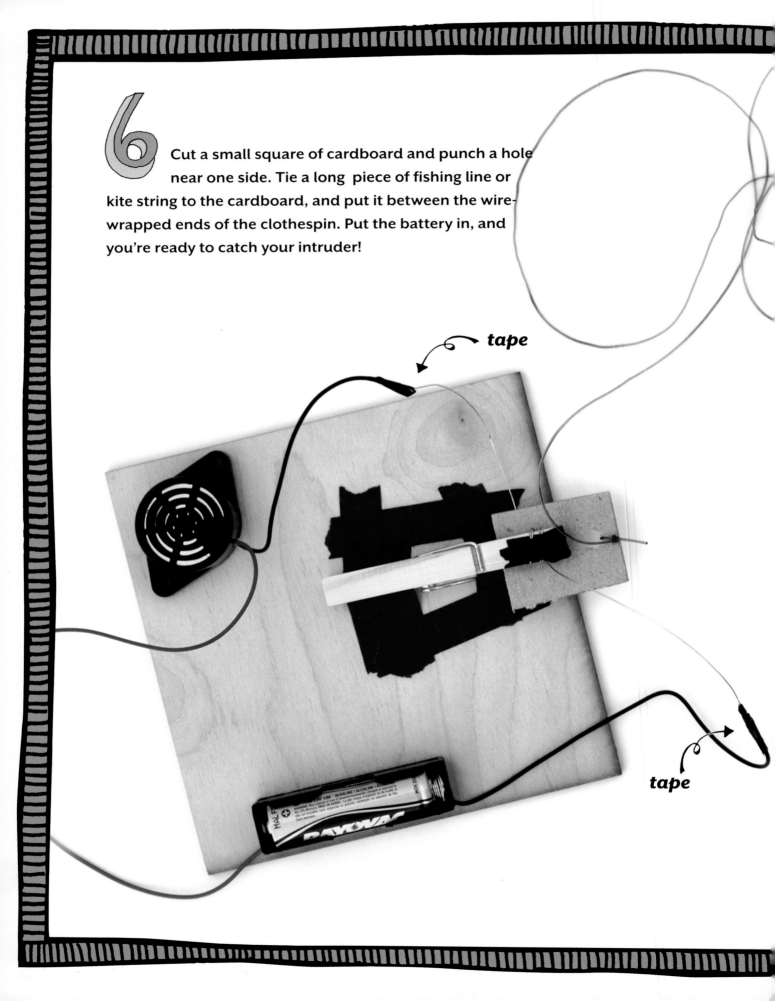

6 Cut a small square of cardboard and punch a hole near one side. Tie a long piece of fishing line or kite string to the cardboard, and put it between the wire-wrapped ends of the clothespin. Put the battery in, and you're ready to catch your intruder!

tape

tape

7 String the fishing line across the door to your room by setting the alarm on one side of the doorframe and taping the end of the string to the opposite side of the doorframe. If the door opens or someone steps through, they'll trigger the line and the alarm will sound!

YAY!

You made it to the final step: the FUN step!

GOTCHA!

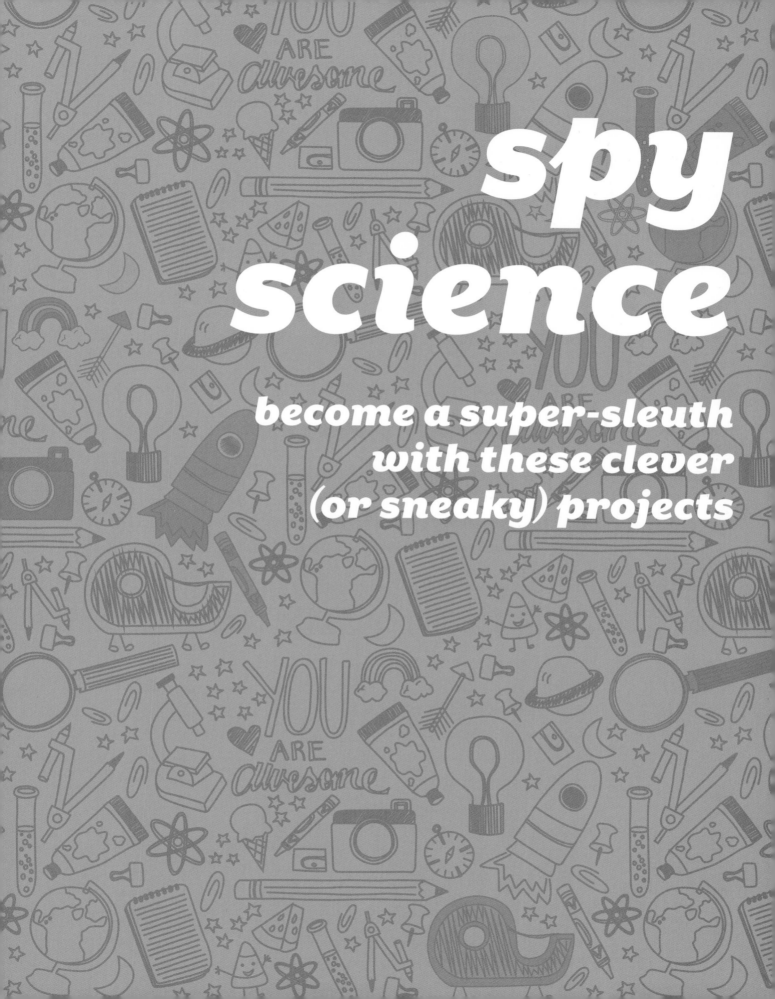

spy
science

become a super-sleuth with these clever (or sneaky) projects

chromatography

Chromatography is a Greek word!

Chroma means "color" and graphien means "to write"

Chromatography is used as a tool to study evidence; it works by separating mixtures. Forensic scientists—those who work to solve a crime—use chromatography to analyze ink samples. Different inks are made of different colors. We can separate the colors in an ink to see if the same ink was used on two different documents or if someone forged a document or signature.

1 Color around the top edges of a coffee filter. Loosely bunch it up at the center and place it in a shallow cup of water.

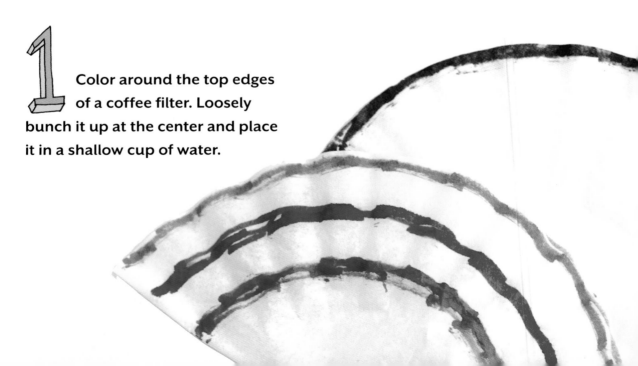

After a few minutes, the colors will start to run, or "bleed."

Take the filter out, and lay it flat to dry.

You can see the inks separating. The purple has developed fuzzy arms of magenta and blue at the edges.

components of blood

You already know from your scrapes and cuts that you have blood running through your body. It's very important! Learn about the four components of blood and what each part does to keep you healthy.

Just mix the ingredients together!

The four components of blood

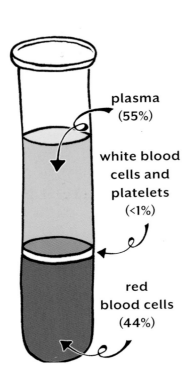

plasma (55%)

white blood cells and platelets (<1%)

red blood cells (44%)

- *red blood cells (44% of blood volume) = candy red hots*
  Red blood cells carry oxygen and carbon dioxide around the body. They live for only about 3 months but are continuously produced in the bone marrow.
- *plasma (55% of blood volume) = corn syrup*
  This is a thick, clear-yellowish liquid that carries dissolved food and waste through the body.
- *white blood cells (.5% of blood volume) = miniature marshmallows*
  These are oddly shaped and bigger than red blood cells. White blood cells "eat" bits of old blood cells and attack germs.
- *platelets (.5% of blood volume) = candy sprinkles*
  Platelets help clot your blood— very important! —they make a scab when you have a scrape.

In a drop of blood the size of this pin, there are:

- *5,000,000 red blood cells*
- *10,000 white blood cells*
- *250,000 platelets*

cool

did you know?

There are four types of blood, and whatever type yours is, it was inherited from your parents. You can ask them if they know what type you have! Each type can be positive or negative—so A positive or A negative, for example.

Type A has...
A antigens in red blood cells and anti-B antibodies in plasma.

Type B has...
B antigens in red blood cells and anti-A antibodies in plasma.

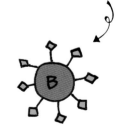

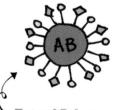

Type AB has...
A and B antigens in red blood cells and no antibodies in plasma.

AB is the least common type!

Type O has...
No antigens in red blood cells and anti-A and anti-B antibodies in plasma.

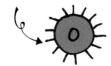

O is the most common type!

diy dna

DNA is the material that contains the genetic code for all living things. DNA determines how an organism will look and function. In humans, it determines hair and eye color, for example.

When stretched out, DNA looks like a twisted double-ladder—you'll see here when you make it—and it is actually called a double helix.

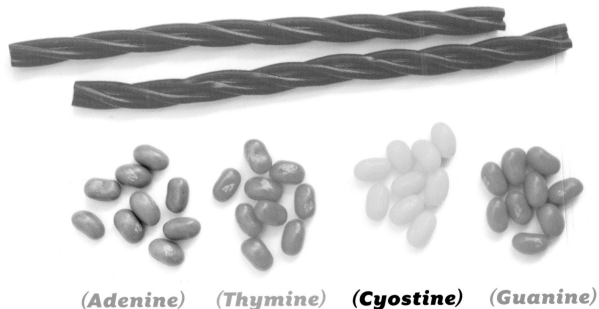

(Adenine)   (Thymine)   **(Cyostine)**   (Guanine)

There are four types of chemical bases in DNA.
Adenine (A), Thymine (T), **Cyostine** (C), and Guanine (G).

They always form pairs in very specific ways.
Adenine (A) always pairs with Thymine (T).
Cyostine (C) always pairs with Guanine (G).

Before you get started,
color and write in your jellybean color choices here! This will help you keep track and make sure you are pairing your chemical bases correctly.

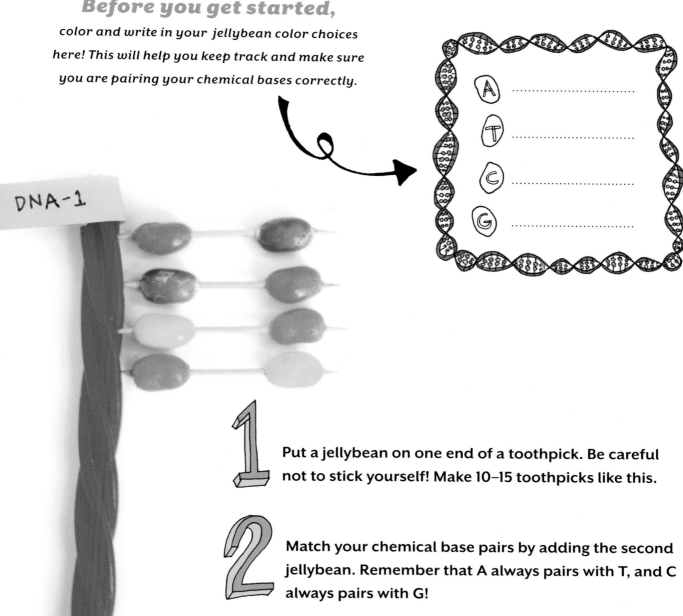

DNA-1

1 Put a jellybean on one end of a toothpick. Be careful not to stick yourself! Make 10–15 toothpicks like this.

2 Match your chemical base pairs by adding the second jellybean. Remember that A always pairs with T, and C always pairs with G!

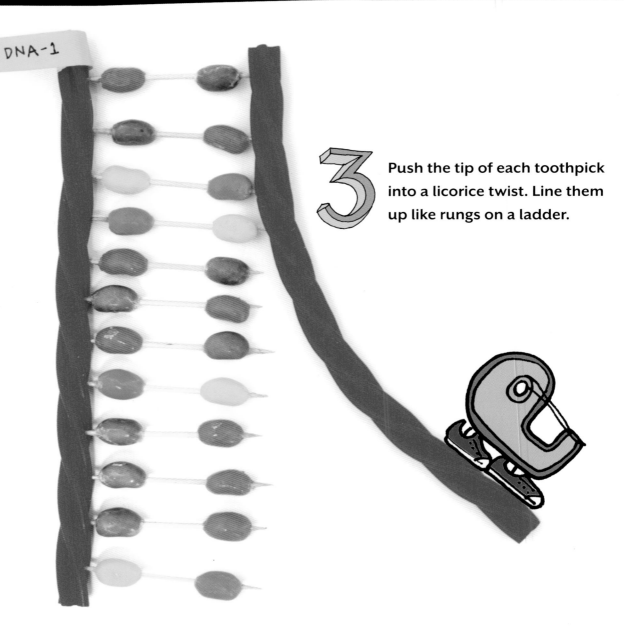

DNA-1

3 Push the tip of each toothpick into a licorice twist. Line them up like rungs on a ladder.

4 Now add the second licorice twist along the other side. Carefully press the tips of the toothpicks into the licorice. Give it a twist to see the shape of a double helix.

You've made a GIANT model of DNA!

5 fun + funky facts
about DNA

- If you unwrapped all of the DNA you have in all of your cells, you could reach the moon 600 times!
- Every human being shares 99% of their DNA with every other human.
- A parent and child share 99.5% of the same DNA.
- Humans and chimpanzees have 98% of their DNA in common.
- Humans and cabbage share about 40–50% of the same DNA. Uh, whaaaa?

This is the stuff we're made of!

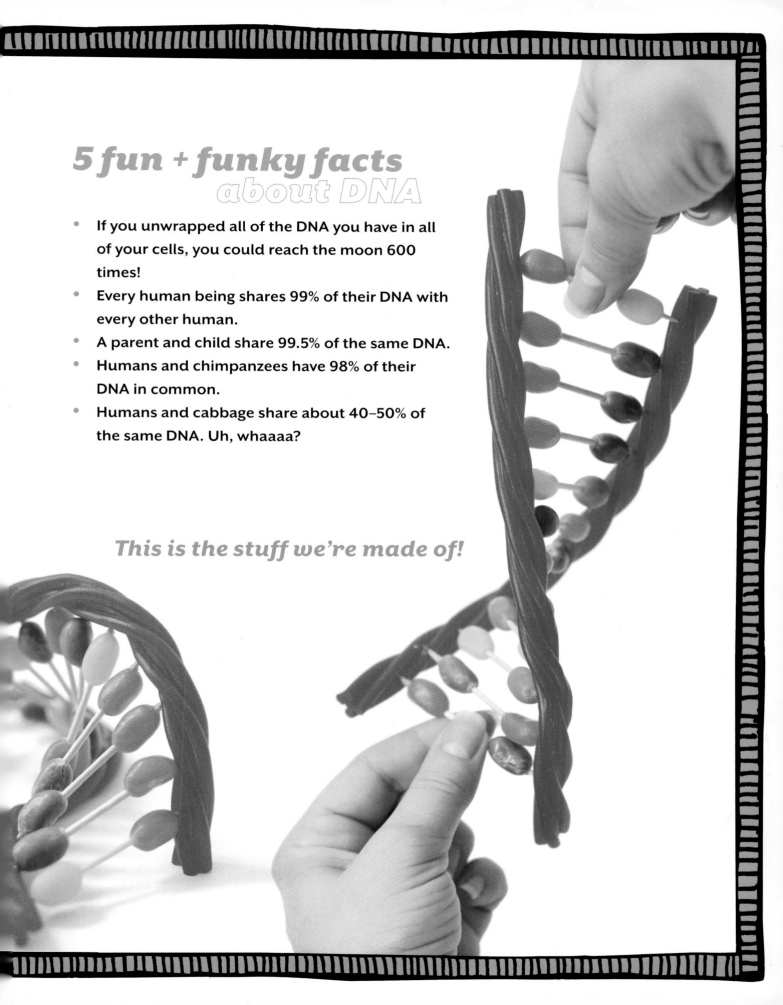

dna extraction

You can extract some DNA from a living thing . . .

maker checklist

⅓ cup of water

2 tsp. liquid dish detergent

1 tsp. sea salt

4 ripe strawberries

sealable plastic baggie

kitchen funnel

square of cheesecloth

small bowl + jar/cup

2 test tubes

rubbing alcohol, chilled

thin wooden skewer

It's easier than you think! Here we used a strawberry, but you can also use an onion or grapes. You can even extract your own DNA from a bit of your saliva mixed with a salty solution like Gatorade.

You will be able to see the strawberry DNA separate out of your mashed-up mixture. It looks like white goo.

1 Mix together the dish soap, water, and sea salt in a small bowl, and set it aside. This is your extraction liquid.

A·maz·ing

2 Trim your strawberries and put them in a sealable plastic baggie. Squeeze them with your hands until the strawberries are all mashed up.

3 Add 3 tablespoons of the extraction liquid to the strawberries in the bag. Reseal the bag and squeeze again for another minute.

did you know?

The liquid detergent will help break the strawberry cells open, allowing the DNA to spill out. The salt helps create an environment where the different strands of DNA can gather in a clump, making it easier for you to see.

4 Line the funnel with the cheesecloth, and set it over a jar. Pour the strawberry mixture in and let it sit so that the liquid drips through. Pour this liquid into a test tube.

5 Now carefully and slowly pour an equal amount of the chilled rubbing alcohol into the test tube. You do *not* want it to slosh in quickly. Tilting the test tube helps!

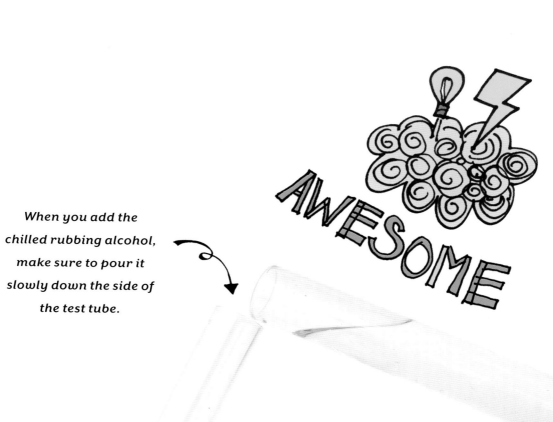

When you add the chilled rubbing alcohol, make sure to pour it slowly down the side of the test tube.

AWESOME

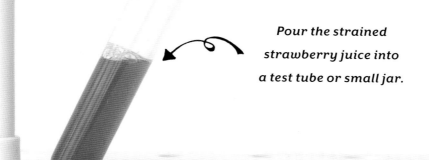

Pour the strained strawberry juice into a test tube or small jar.

6 Let your mixture sit. You will see the strawberry's DNA rise up out of the red mixture and into the clear alcohol. Cool!

Curious Janes in our Weird Science Workshop extracted DNA from grapes. Grapes were way harder to mash up than strawberries! What will you try?

7 Dip the wooden skewer into the solution and catch some of the white goop. This is the DNA!

SUPERFUN

GRAPES!

invisible ink

Squeeze a lemon to make a secret message

maker checklist

1 lemon, squeezed!

water

cotton swab

sheet of white paper

sun, iron, or light bulb

When life gives you lemons . . .
make a secret message!

1 Add a spoonful of water to the juice of one lemon. Mix gently.

2 Dip the cotton swab into the juice and write a secret message on your paper. Let it dry completely so that the message is invisible.

3 To share your secret, set the paper in the hot sun or hold it close to a light bulb. You can also iron the paper (with adult help) to reveal it.

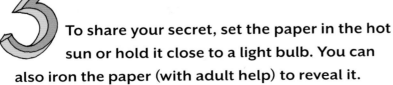

P.S. Photographing invisible ink is **REALLY** tricky! This is what our message said after it was revealed.

did you know?

Lemon juice is an organic substance that *oxidizes* and turns brown when it is heated up.

Diluting, or adding water, to the lemon juice makes it very hard to see when you apply it to the paper. No one will notice that your secret is there until the paper is heated and the message is revealed!

Other substances that work in the same way are orange juice, honey, milk, onion juice, vinegar, and wine. Invisible ink can also be made using chemical reactions or by viewing certain liquids in ultraviolet (UV) light.

dusting for fingerprints

We leave our fingerprints on everything we touch, and, because each fingerprint is different, we can use them to identify people. Forensic scientists lift fingerprints from crime scenes to help them determine who was there. You can try this, too!

maker checklist

cocoa powder or chalk dust

clear tape

a small, soft paint brush

1 Find or make a fingerprint (you could hold a cup or bowl, or press your hand against a window).

We used a butter knife to shave a bit of dust from old summer sidewalk chalk.

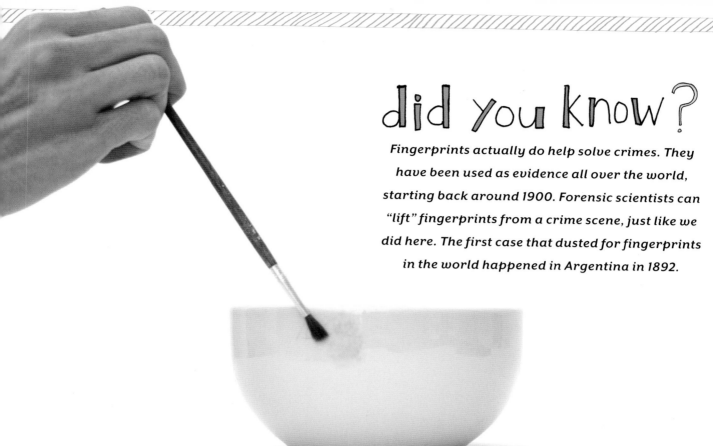

did you know?

Fingerprints actually do help solve crimes. They have been used as evidence all over the world, starting back around 1900. Forensic scientists can "lift" fingerprints from a crime scene, just like we did here. The first case that dusted for fingerprints in the world happened in Argentina in 1892.

2 Dip your brush into chalk or cocoa powder and dust it over the fingerprint. Blow gently to clear away the extra powder. The dust will stick to the grease on the fingerprint.

3 Press a piece of clear tape on the print, and carefully peel it off. You've lifted the fingerprint!

diy your room

cool, colorful projects to spruce up your space

glitter jars

save a few jars from the recycling bin and make your own sparkly containers

make
your
own

maker checklist

clean glass jars

white glue

lots and lots of glitter!

foam brushes

a few plastic plates

stir stick or spoon

1 Fill your jar with about ½ inch of glue. Add plenty of glitter and stir it up in the bottom of the jar.

2 Use a foam brush to spread the glitter all over the inside of the jar. You can also mix the glue and glitter on a plastic plate with a stir stick and spoon and paint from that instead.

3 Turn your jar upside down on a plastic plate to let any extra glue run out. After about 10 minutes, turn the jar right-side up. Add more glittery glue to any spots that need it, then let it dry.

watercolor pillows

maker checklist

white pillow insert

colorful permanent markers

rubbing alcohol

pipette or spray bottle

dryer

We colored directly on a white pillow insert! You could also use a white pillowcase.

4 quick tips for an awesome pillow!

- Before you start, test your colors on a corner of your pillow or a piece of scrap fabric. Some colors "bleed" more than others!
- Plan your design! Your pillow can be abstract (like watercolor or tie-dye) or graphic (like dots or lines). Remember, your color choices are important!
- Make sure to leave some white space to allow your colors to run into each other and mix.
- When you wet your pillow, add the rubbing alcohol slowly and a little at a time. Your pillow should be damp, not soaked!

HOW-TO

1 Cover your work surface with a plastic tablecloth or large garbage bag.

2 Curate your palette by selecting permanent markers in your favorite colors.

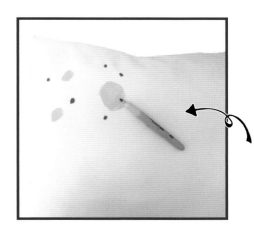

3 Draw on your pillow with the markers. The more ink you use, the more the color will run or bleed.

4 Saturate your pillow with rubbing alcohol. Use a pipette to drop water or a spray bottle to mist, and watch the magic happen!

5 Let your pillow fully dry, and run it through the dryer to seal in your design.

screen printing

Screen printing is our new favorite project! You might think you'll need special tools and complicated techniques, but it's really quite simple!

maker checklist

silk screen-printing mesh or a pair of thin tights

6- or 8-inch embroidery hoop

permanent marker

newspaper

decoupage medium

small bowl + paint brush

large piece of cotton canvas or thick art paper

small piece of cardboard or foam core

screen printing paints

what is screen printing?

Screen printing is a method of printing in which ink or paint is forced through a fine mesh screen onto a surface. It's a way to make an image and then *replicate* it, or repeat the same image many times. You probably have lots of T-shirts and tote bags that have been screen-printed.

You can find these paints for screen printing on fabric at any arts store or online—we used Speedball brand, and we chose brights + neons!

1 Design your stencil.

The first step is to create a good, clear stencil—pick a simple shape that does not use a lot of lines for detail. We used fun fruit shapes!

2 Create your frame.

Place the silk mesh or tights into the embroidery hoop and tighten it so that it fits snugly.

Lay the frame screen-side down over your stencil, and trace the shape with a permanent marker.

leave the positive areas, or the main picture, clear

cover the negative areas, or the background space, with decoupage medium

3 Mask your screen.

Turn the frame screen-side up and set it on newspaper to catch drips. Brush the decoupage medium onto all the areas that are *not* part of your shape. This is called *masking*.

A·maz·ing

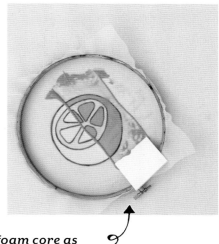

we used a bit of foam core as our "squeegee"

4

Add paint and print!

Set the frame screen-side down on the canvas and spoon a little paint onto it. Hold the frame down firmly and, using a bit of cardboard as your squeegee, drag the paint across your design with a little pressure. Go back and forth a few times to cover the whole shape. Peel the frame off the canvas and see your print!

tip: You can print the same design in different paints! Just gently wash and dry your screen in between colors.

for framing your piece

4 12-inch strips model-making wood or
   colorful cardboard (or paint stir sticks!)
masking tape + double-stick tape (or glue)
2 large (2- or 3-inch) bulldog clips
colorful cord or string for hanging
optional:
markers
needle + thread in coordinating color

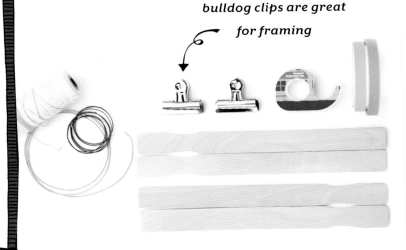

*bulldog clips are great
for framing*

5 Frame it! Hang it!

To add a simple frame, sandwich the top and bottom of your artwork between two strips of model-making wood or colorful cardboard. Use masking tape and double stick tape, or glue, to secure it. Clip two large bulldog clips at the top and run a piece of pretty cord through them.

Our canvas is long and thin (12 x 28 inches) so paint stir sticks from the local hardware store worked perfectly for us!

Embellish!

You can embellish your artwork with color fabric markers or a bit of stitching. Just a touch will do! For example: a subtle accent of orange marker at the lemon's edge. Don't be afraid to try different tools and play around with the materials. You'll learn a lot and figure out better ways to make your prints!

paint chip calendar

maker checklist

frame

paint chips

scissors + glue

washi tape

chalk paint markers

1 Grab a simple frame, pick your favorite paint chip palette, and spend a little time cutting and measuring for a fabulous result!

2
Edge your calendar with washi tape and write on it with chalk-paint markers so you can erase and reuse it each month!

snow globes

Snow globes are a fun, easy project with a totally awesome take-away. Find glycerin (liquid soap) and oven-bake clay at any good craft store.

maker checklist

oven-bake clay

oven

glass jar with lid

hot glue gun

water

¼ cup glycerin

glitter + sequins

1 Make a colorful creation using oven-bake clay—just make sure it will fit through the mouth of your jar before baking! Bake the clay following package instructions—usually at 250° for 15 minutes for every ¼ inch of thickness. Remove carefully and cool!

2 Glue your design to the inside lid of the jar. Please ask a grown-up to help you with the hot glue gun!

3 Fill your jar about ¾ of the way with water. Add a big squirt of glycerin (about ¼ cup) and a handful of glitter and sparkles. Then put the lid on tightly, and give it a little shake. You've got your snow globe!

We filled our snow globe to the brim with a colorful cityscape, tons of sequins and sparkles, and—yep!— even Junior Ghost.

hula hoop rug

Turn old tees into a super soft rug—it will be your favorite spot to sit or rest your feet.

maker checklist

24- or 36-inch hula hoop

lots of colorful T-shirts

good fabric scissors

Before you start . . .

Grab a couple plastic hoops from the dollar store—one for weaving and one for doing the hula! Pick your palette before you begin!

Turn a hula hoop into a loom!

A *loom* is a device used to weave cloth. A loom holds "warp" threads or strands under tension to help weave the "weft" threads in. Read on to find out what these terms mean!

tip: This project can take a long time depending on the size of your rug (or cushion, or whatever you make!). You can work on it little by little whenever you need to busy your hands.

1 Lay the shirt flat, and cut strips straight across; stop when you reach the arms (save the top part for tassels).

Don't worry about jagged edges—they will completely disappear!

MAKE
COOL
THINGS

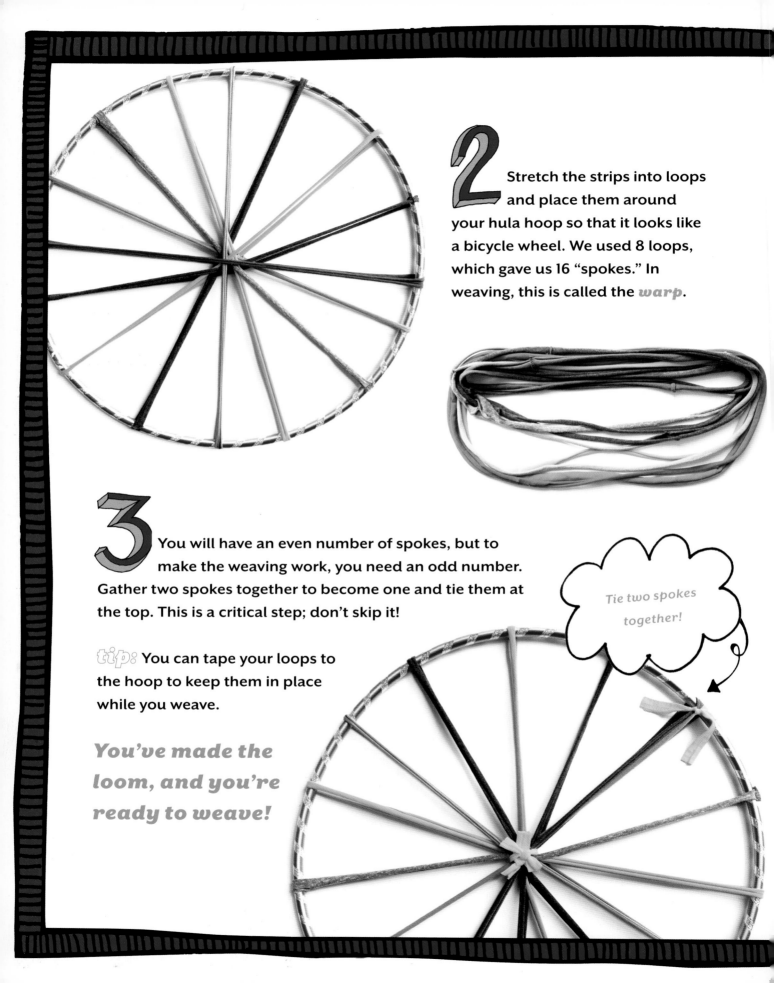

2 Stretch the strips into loops and place them around your hula hoop so that it looks like a bicycle wheel. We used 8 loops, which gave us 16 "spokes." In weaving, this is called the *warp*.

3 You will have an even number of spokes, but to make the weaving work, you need an odd number. Gather two spokes together to become one and tie them at the top. This is a critical step; don't skip it!

tip: You can tape your loops to the hoop to keep them in place while you weave.

You've made the loom, and you're ready to weave!

Tie two spokes together!

4 Cut the rest of your loops so you have long strips of fabric for weaving. This is called the *weft*. Tie your first strip around the bundle of spokes at the middle of your wheel. Pick any spot to start weaving. Weave over one spoke and under the next.

tip: Push the weft toward the center as you go so the rug is nice and thick, but don't pull it too tightly or you will end up with a bowl!

Over, under, over, under.

5 When you reach the end of your strip, tie another to it and keep weaving. When you get further from the center, weave over and under each *piece* of the spoke loop.

tip: Leave at least 6 inches of space between your weaving and the hula hoop so you have enough room to tie off the spokes.

6 When you're done weaving, tie the end of your last strip around a few neighboring loops to secure it. Cut your spokes near the hula hoop, loop the ends around a few inches of the weaving, and tie securely.

To take the weaving off the loom, cut here.

Try it!

t-shirt pillows

make your own

maker checklist

favorite old graphic tee

ruler + chalk, for measuring

good scissors

pillow insert or fiber filler

1 Lay your shirt flat and draw a neat rectangle (using chalk and a ruler) around the design. Use as much of the T-shirt as you can.

2 Carefully cut out your design. Cut a matching rectangle from the back of the same T-shirt *or* a T-shirt of a different color.

3 Lay the pieces on top of each other so you can cut both at the same time. First, cut 2-inch squares from each corner. Then cut ½-inch-wide strips around all the sides.

4 Starting at one corner, tie each pair of strips together with a double-knot. Go around 3 sides of the T-shirt. Before tying the last side, stuff your pillow with fiber filler or a pillow insert. Close it up with the rest of the knots and . . .

. . . show it off on your bed!

meet Curious Jane

CURIOUS JANE

is for girls ages 6 to 11 who like to make things! Everything we do revolves around *science* + *design* + *engineering*.

We run summer camps and workshops in and around New York City, and we publish a print magazine so that girls everywhere can have the Curious Jane experience at home!

We empower girls through hands-on, project-based learning, and we always have fun!

get more Curious Jane!

Curious Jane Magazine—full of fun stuff to do and make!

Hands-on projects and DIY fun for girls everywhere! It's high-quality, ad-free, and packed full of clever stuff to do and make. It's as smart as it is fun. Subscribe for your daughter or give it as a gift: *www.curiousjanemagazine.com*

For details about our programs and workshops, visit *www.curiousjanecamp.com*

Would you like to bring Curious Jane to your area? Drop us an email! We always enjoy growing and collaborating in interesting ways: *info@curiousjanecamp.com*

about us

We're a small but passionate team, we love what we do, and we want the girls to love it, too! In 2014, we were thrilled to receive a prestigious Mission Main Street Small Business Grant from Chase Bank in support of our programs for girls. That grant allowed us to grow in new ways. Each year, we offer more workshops, add new locations, and work with amazing organizations. In 2015, we launched our print magazine so that girls can try our projects at home. We are excited to grow the Curious Jane community!

meet the Makers

Samantha . . .

founded Curious Jane eight years ago to give her daughters, and all girls, a chance to be creative and inventive in a high-energy space. She's Southern-raised, now Brooklyn-based (with design degrees from Yale and Pratt). She loves to tinker, make, create and—of course!!—do tons of fun stuff around NYC and the world with her girls, family, and friends. If she won the lottery and quit her job, she would . . . *whaaaaat?!?!* She'd never quit her job. Ever. She loves it and counts herself super lucky to wake up each morning jazzed about everything the day will bring her.

[Her mini-makers are Eleanor, age 15, and Olivia, age 12.]

Melisa . . .

works on marketing, outreach, strategic connections, and new ways to extend the Curious Jane brand. Originally from Texas, she's now happy to call Brooklyn her home. She loves to travel, laugh, think big, and cook. She's inspired by the creativity and ingenuity of the Curious Jane girls and appreciates that spark in both of her children—a daughter who attends the programs and a son who takes interest in the entrepreneurial aspects of the business. She isn't shy when it comes to opinions or red lipstick and loves sharing the Curious Jane mission with girls (like you!) everywhere.

[Her mini-makers are Jasper, age 12, and Magnolia, age 10.]

Elissa . . .

does all things design—and at Curious Jane, that is a lot! She styles the projects and doodles the illustrations for the magazine; she creates the visual presence online and in print; and she sets her magic wand to Curious Jane projects, parties, and workspaces! She loves trampoline parks, traveling, decorating birthday cakes, and making up silly games with her three kids. She is so grateful to live, work, and dream in Brooklyn. Riding her bright-yellow bicycle to Curious Jane headquarters is her favorite way to start the day.

[Her mini-makers are Leo, age 10, Ezra, age 8, and Sylvie, age 6.]

favorite tools + materials

permanent markers

rubber cement (a must for working with paper)

craft foam (regular and self-adhesive)

oven-bake clay

glitter (yep . . . we love it!)

wiggly eyes (adds personality to any project)

GOOD construction paper (a must! Our favorite is made by Blick Art Materials—it's inexpensive and has great color and quality)

hole punches in different shapes and sizes

good, sharp scissors for paper and for fabric (Fiskars brand are great)

foam core sheets

LEDs and coin batteries (in size C2032)

mini pager motors

bulk or remnant packs of ribbons and fabric bits

cool containers in all sizes (save them and make something!)

all the tapes!

washi tape

colorful masking tape

neon duct tape

double-sided tape

sticky dots

foam tape

resources

Adafruit Industries supplies sewn-in circuits and other accessible, specialty electronics.

Blick Art Materials provides an enormous and excellent selection of art and craft supplies (the Dick Blick brand is inexpensive, high-quality, and great for students).

Carolina Biological Supply Company provides science lab items, like test tubes, pipettes, and critters to dissect!

CreateForLess is an affordable crafting supplier.

Discount School Supply ® is great for quantity packs of pom-poms, pipe cleaners, sparkles, wiggly eyes, etc. Super economical!

Hobby Engineering is an online retailer for gears, motors, and other tinkering supplies.

Ryonet ® screen-prints mesh, among other materials.

SparkFun provides specialty electronic components and has an easy-to-use website.

Steve Spangler Science is a source for super-fun science project supplies.